Stirring the Soup

William Doreski

Copyright© 2020 William Doreski
ISBN: 978-93-90202-44-7

First Edition: 2020
Rs. 200/-

Cyberwit.net
HIG 45 Kaushambi Kunj, Kalindipuram
Allahabad - 211011 (U.P.) India
http://www.cyberwit.net
Tel: +(91) 9415091004 +(91) (532) 2552257
E-mail: info@cyberwit.net

Printed at Repro India Limited.

In Memory of James and Joanne Randall

The sleep in your eye like a bee on a rose

Frank Stanford, "Night Time"

Permit me voyage, love, into your hands.

Hart Crane, "Voyages III"

Some of these poems have appeared in *Abbreviate, Bindweed, Bombay Review, Cat / Prey, City Key, Consequence, Courtship of Winds, Drunken Llama, Empty Sink, Euonia, Flare, Fishbowl, Forage, Ground Fresh Thursday, Hamilton Stone Review, Home Planet News, Jazz Cigarette, Literary Yard, Literature Today, Little Dog Poetry, Lunaris, Lunate, The Machinery, Misfit, Modern Poetry Quarterly Review, Muddy River Poetry Review, November Bees, Otoliths, Oxford Magazine, Peacock Journal, Poet Lore, Poetry Porch, Poetry Repair, Pyrokinection, Randomly Accessed Poetics, Riding Light, Sewer Lid, Slant, Split Rock, Starwheel, Truck, Vintage Poetry, White Ash, The Wire's Dream,* and *Wildflower Muse.* Many thanks to the editors of these journals.

Contents

1.

Fishing in the Charles

Claw-footing stone to stone
in shallows, indifferent
to runners, dog-walkers, us,
a great blue heron rummages
for fish for a midday snack.

As we watch, it spears and scissors
a perch, hoists and swallows it
in a long undulant gesture
of unfolded neck. Hardly
a ripple marks the site. The staid

geometry of MIT
across the river looks aghast,
but it always does. Behind us,
the Prudential Center towers
prop themselves against the clouds.

Such an urban frame to feature
such a primal event. We nod
to acknowledge the heron's skill,
its adaptive style, the S-bend
of neck, prehensile stick-legs

that hardly seem to part water,
the wings folded like tissue.
The grace of this heron punctuates
with diacritical urgency,
but almost no one has noticed

the uncommon sighting;
and only we have paused to note
how easily that fish went down
and consider how bottomless
the place it now inhabits.

Tulips on Commonwealth Avenue

Giant footfall prowls the city.
Bass notes of traffic quake tulips
on the north side of the avenue.
We admire the plantings arranged
by height and color, the labor
of gardeners hired to flatter
citizens more equal than us.
A professor claims we've discovered
twenty percent of the species
evolved to compete with us.
The rest will go extinct without
the grace of Latin names. I touch
the back of your neck and sense
power throbbing in varied shades
of melon, apple, and clementine.
You could be anthropomorphic—
a Renaissance figure made of fruit.
You could ripen so abruptly
the burst of flavor would sate
the entire city at once. Teasing
this notion of taste, inspired
by the huddles of tulips brimming
in tiny manicured front yards,
suggests how deeply we're rooted.
This depth makes passing strangers
shy away in case affection
gets infectious and the trembling
underground erupts with flowers
no one has ever seen before.

Their colors would astonish us
with yellow and crimson edged
by pure blue flame so overwrought
it could render us all one species
equally subject to extinction
and prone to mutations of love.

Angles / Angels

The angle at which our bodies
meets our souls has stiffened high
in the upper atmosphere where
birds petrify and enter orbit
with a minimum of squawks
and cackles. From ground level,
peering without binoculars
into a great sweep of sun-drift,
we conclude that the mating
of distinct philosophies has failed.

Morning bristles. Woodpeckers
hammer the suet cakes we placed
in locations shielded from hawks.
Wild turkeys scratch for grubs,
their poults fuzzy as fiddleheads.
Bumblebees fluster hydrangea.
We keep looking up although
we can't see but only infer
those orbiting fossilized birds
that may, in fact, be angels.

Angel or angle, the plain
trigonometry that shapes us
locates itself on paper maps
no one can read anymore.
We lack the proper instruments
to resurvey familiar scenes,
so we drink coffee the color

of the recent floods in Texas
and discuss whether our lack
of future has calmed or numbed us.

The news every day is bad.
Crashes and fire kill neighbors,
politicians scandalize sex,
Antarctica breaks off in chunks.
The smell of decaying wood
rises from clammy forests
and from sultry city basements
to deter angels from alighting
and to further splay the angles
at which our variations meet.

This Autumnal Suspense

Looking down on feeding ducks
from the Public Garden bridge
we note their dip and bobble,
tail-up, paddling, as personal
as climbing in or out of the bath.
The pedaled swan boats smooth along
without disturbing the ducks.
We bask like marble effigies
of ourselves. The September sun
belies the churning of the tropics,
which will cough up a storm to smelt
this garden under gouts of rain
and smite it with seesaws of wind.
The ducks will huddle in the dark
under the bridge. No one will feed them
popcorn, the paddle boats docked
and roped against wayward tides.
Later walking home we'll watch
the mansard roofs shed weather
the way some people shed their lovers.
Edging the garden, the streets crawl
on all fours, bearing heavy traffic
with Atlas-like patience. We leave
the ducks to their crumbs and stroll
with Parisian confidence. Grown old
from a safe distance, we regard
each other with opiate glances.
The walkway shudders as forces

knot and kink underground,
deeper than the ducks can dive—
deeper than we're willing to plumb.

La Farge Blue

In Trinity Church we wander
to the altar, then turn to admire
light shivering through the blue,

bottomless blue, that La Farge
embodied in the windows
placed high above the vestibule

to absorb the afternoon sun.
Braced in gloomy stone the blaze
of this implacable color frames

Jesus with two marble pillars
too formal to support the plain
colloquial ministry he preached.

But they hold and focus our gaze
for long moments, infusing
the blue deeply inside us.

Slumped in a pew we avoid
addressing each other until
the heavens stop revolving.

The whole afternoon creeps forward
with a slow nervous movement.
What if blasphemous stones fell

and broke these elegant windows?
Would we still regard each other
with a deep-set silence impossible

for the organ to violate?
Are we ready to slip outside?
The windows further deepen.

The autumn sun has lowered
behind the Prudential Tower,
which thrusts into an atmosphere

breathed by ordinary people
among whom we'll shine discreetly
with colors they've yet to explore.

An All-Russian Program

In Symphony Hall the small notes
champagne to the ceiling and burst.
The large ones clop down the aisle
on imaginary horses, grinning
despite their tragic implications.
In your nine-dollar seat you absorb
Shostakovich ripening with age,
Tchaikovsky fidgeting minor chords,
Rachmaninoff slamming the door
on movement after movement.

The orchestra excites itself
in several dimensions. The crowd
staggers as the all-Russian program
with its bluff Tsarist overtones
rumbles out the big doors and stops
traffic on Huntington Avenue.
In the sweep of the coda one button
pops from the conductor's jacket
and lands in the second row.

You clutch your program to your chest
and stroll into the afternoon
where cloud-cover has bruised itself
on a hurricane far out at sea.
The stopped traffic has snarled. Two cops
struggle to get it moving again.
One large piano note left over
from Rachmaninoff lies on the walk,
having tumbled from its horse.

You want to stash it in your tote bag
as a souvenir, but fear that like
a sparrow it would die of fright.
A wonder no one has stepped on it.
But safe in the bowels of the subway
you wish you'd snatched that stray note,
although in your small apartment
it might have resurrected
so loudly the neighbors would wince
and your lone tall window shatter,
exposing you to a draught.

Glacial Erratics in Belmont

Being rocks, they don't remember.
Or remember very little.

The streets square up to houses,
to the playground, tennis courts,

and the large but effete cemetery.
The rocks squat self-conscious

on lawns as tough and polished
as the law allows. I kneel

before one and feel its cold
shoulders try to shrug me off.

The householders often catch
rock-worshippers like me

leaning into their property,
but almost never call the police.

Glacial erratics are common
in the Boston Basin, their weight

much of what holds us together.
I would like to stroke the surface

of these three fine examples,
but don't want to actually trespass

without theology to back me.
The cool dusk pools in the street.

The cries of kids in the playground
recede like an ebbing surf.

I'll take photos to prove that these rocks
thrive in this plain old suburb.

And then I'll wander off with hands
roughened by imagining that

I've spent a lifetime worshipping
stone that hardly ever responds.

King's Chapel Bell

Ringing the King's Chapel bell,
the largest Paul Revere cast,
you leap at the rope and drag
with all your weight and suffer
reverberations that fill you

with the shock of sudden love.
From a safe, empathic distance
I picture you dangling with both
hands on the rope, the clang
assuming a dozen dimensions,

the bronze so thoroughly beaten
it's too tough to respond to you
the way I do, with clapper subdued.
You like the taste of my jokes,
sometimes, but ringing the bell

is serious enough to impale
the silence we've let ripen
between us: impale and spill
blood that's thinner than water.
That reminds me how the rain

clatters on the chapel roof
in several languages, mostly
ecclesiastical of intent.
We can't interpret but we claim
a heritage derived from bronze

and granite, leaded glass and oak,
and mistake it for religion.
No one believes in the post
Episcopal God who haunts
this Unitarian space; but

watching you yank the ropes
to evoke that tremendous sound
I believe in you so perfectly
that even the rain's conversation
for a moment seems almost true.

2.

Among the Animals

On the Athenaeum's fifth floor
in your favorite red leather chair—
the only one compact enough
to cuddle your thighs—you read
Wind in the Willows with bright eyes
shivering across the pages.

Scholars tucked into alcoves
shudder over massive insights
that unfolded on their laptops
are certain to solve the planet.
They should don the square paper hats
of Newtonians just for fun.

They should hoot and toot like Toad
sputtering in the dust of autos.
They should note how poised you pose
in that red leather chair positioned
to face the length of the building.
Certain standards of intellect

apply to the slightest gestures—
the re-shelving of books, the flip
of a page of one's notebook,
the tick-tock of computer keys
as a dissertation unfolds
one endnote after another.

Rat and Mole and Toad require
a stable natural environment,
which beyond these tempered walls
has fractured into photographs
too carelessly framed to survive.
Your red chair props you against

the city's onrush. The old gray light
exuded from puritan graves
is faint but still tough enough
to choke those unwary folks
who haven't found cushy seating
and something golden to read.

A Portrait of Lafayette

by Samuel F.B. Morse. The tough
old potato head rendered
in earth tones makes us cringe.
Around us the slightly fey
elegance of the Athenaeum
consolidates about a view
of the Granary Burying Ground
where tourists clump about graves
of Hancock, Revere, and Mother Goose.

We've haunted these places for years,
but facing down the hero
of the revolution depicted
by the telegraph's inventor
we merge like overlapping shadows
and become a single entity.
Why this realistic portrait
should catalyze and confirm
our singularity baffles me;
but as we browse the exhibit,
then move to the upper floors
where the stolid books outflank us,
we lean into our whispers
with increasingly sultry passions
only Henry James could sort.

But we can't live in a novel,
not even in this library
with its sunny views and marble

sculpture posed to encourage us.
We elevate from floor to floor
and examine the ranks of books
and wish we could read them all,
wish we could read each other,
read the entity we've become
without having to turn the pages
and risk what's written beyond.

Your White Dress Adrift

Dreaming your white dress adrift
flimsy without you in it
troubles me in earth-tones deep

enough to soil that dainty garment
and stifle your wandering spirit
before it settles inside me.

In the archive your papers gleam
like metal after a plane crash.
I rustle them so loudly

the librarian cries in protest
and sends me to the coffee shop
to caffeinate and calm myself.

Someone asks if I ever dream
of sexual urges prevailing
over vague scholarly distance.

No one can picture you naked,
if that's what's implied. Your dress
flits about without you, but you

don't exist outside of it. Snow
braces the first week of spring,
stifling daffodils and crocuses

that imagine swaths of sunlight
imperial enough to sustain.
I'm as firmly rooted as they are;

but when your white dress appears
I rave into myself and retract
every attempt to embalm you.

The Grace of the Garden Cemetery

In August we elongate
to conform to certain shadows
no particular object casts.
The streets resist interrogation.
The square two-family houses
brace themselves against shifts
in mood and density of cloud.

You walk one route to the bus stop
while I walk another. We meet
in a spangle and jangle of sighs,
wondering where our lives went.
The electric trolley buses hiss
and spark, eager to ingest us,
like being bellied in a whale.

A short ride to the famous
graveyard where we visit famous
and famously rococo graves.
Birds patter along their skyways
with tiny squeaks of pleasure
no human beyond adolescence
can utter without a blush.

We could lie on some heroic grave
and touch both head and foot stones.
But we refrain from blasphemies
against the self-created image
and unpack our picnic lunch

beside a pond so full of turtles
their shells clatter as they swim,

Our ham sandwiches blame us
for their fate, but we eat them
with conscience almost clear, the shape
and color of noon too bluff
and shallow to rebuke us
for hungers we've never curbed.

Resisting the Intelligence

Resting on the edge of the moon
where it grazes the staggered tree line,
I lean into the flavors and drift.
Your room in Paris also overlooks
odors and tastes of varied moods,
but the dead fish haunting the Seine
sour many famous properties
worth many millions of Euros.
You love this clash of decay and chic
in which the city skyline cringes
the way my New England tree line
does, folding into itself
at the first wrinkle of dawn.

So much has yawned itself foolish—
the years we wasted face to face,
the books the library discarded,
the loot from the last Brink's robbery.
Remember the man in the pub
in Forest Hills, who blathered
about that famous crime a week
before it happened? He was the stiff
the cops found locked in a car
behind my Beacon Street apartment.

The moon is barely round enough
to hold my weight. The tree line hurts
by abrading my delicate eyes.
I'd rather be looking at the seam

where your body meets your spirit,
a sea-colored horizon misty
with summer heat. But the autumn
has its way. The ghost of that man
still loiters in the alley, cadging
pennies from anyone who passes.

Paris also features certain ghosts
from the Occupation era
when the blackout prevailed. Soon
it will return, sealing us both
in a gray unlimited vacuum
where we may consort as we please—
the fish-smell dispersing
as we rest our elbows on the moon
in a comforting lack of air.

Days as Heavy as Dinosaurs

Days as heavy as dinosaurs
tend to crush us in their tracks.

Rereading *Ulysses* after
three decades, I feel how softly

time in old Dublin passed when
characters developed themselves

in fiction richer than living.
While I'm turning thick pages

you're raking your favorite leaves,
yellow maples that bandage

every surface like sea-creatures
exposed when the tide goes out.

The weight of the day oppresses
but probably won't kill us.

The northwest wind ruffles
familiar textures, revising

our senses and their grip on things.
I should move indoors with book

and teacup. You should take
a break, fresh leaves swarming the air

like fish in a huge aquarium.
I dreamt that our dead cat returned

to explain the afterlife in terms
simple enough for us to grasp.

I didn't tell you that dream because
we'd both feel crushed a bit flatter

than usual. Too bad the creaking
of wind in the trees isn't speech—

a sermon to reassure us
that someone holds a place for us

in that dining hall in the sky.
Somewhere a diva is singing

the dinosaur song we need to hear
for the sake of our rumpled organs

The footfall passes over us
again and again, but we shrug

our shrugs of a lifetime and work
slowly, surely at our tasks.

For Your Henry James Scrapbook

If I give you a tag of skin
I shed because sunburned reading
The Golden Bowl at Hamden Beach

will you paste it in your scrapbook?
Not your childhood scrapbook
of snapshots and birthday cards

but your Henry James scrapbook
of manuscript fragments and locks
of his thin old hair. Honor me

by preserving this tiny fragment
in an archive long after I've gone
to that vaporous place religion

posits at the end of the road.
Hamden Beach at season's close
remained seductive. Women shaped

like pastries shivered in swimsuits
brighter than the blush of autumn.
Children toppled in surf and screamed

with pleasure, soaking up the last
gasp of summer. I read and read
in my beach chair until I toasted

a lovely sunset pink. The peel
began after the first deep frost,
and now I look like a haunted house

shedding its antique wallpaper.
Let me mail you this rag of hide
You'll laugh because it's transparent

as you always say I become
when pouring myself into books
sensible people find boring.

Boston Salvage

At Boston Salvage we open
at seven to allow the riffraff
to sell us the junk they glean
from Back Bay alleys or steal
from parked cars on Beacon Hill.
Furniture, rugs, clothing, cell phones,
laptops, power tools, copper pipes
liberated from construction sites.

By nine the public has arrived
to bargain. The same dry faces
differently framed. The hot light
of June complicates by casting
shadows through chain-link fencing
to crosshatch expressions and render
everyone a little suspicious
of us, each other, and the world.

Machines from ruined factories,
car parts, lumber stacked outdoors
embellish the intersection
of matter and spirit. From here,
in front of our prefab warehouse,
you can spot the domes and steeples
of famous churches glooming
in the past they helped deform.

You can also count the skyscrapers
marching along Boylston Street,

down through the financial district
toward the harbor where seabirds drift
on the chop and drunken yachtsmen
try to seduce bikinis they've bribed
by flapping their sails and boasting
of salaries larger than Texas.

We at Boston Salvage avoid
any hint of sex in our dealings.
No checks, no credit cards: cash
only, don't ask for an invoice
or receipt. The thick days simper
into dusk the color of dust-storms.
Goods come and go. We pocket
cash for groceries and liquor
and lock the guard dogs in the yard.

Tomorrow will bloom a moment,
splendid with chicory and phlox,
then wither, and the same old trash
will recycle through the premises
like our second or third childhoods,
fourth or even fifth marriages: doomed
by languor, indifference, and rust.

3.

The Paintings in the Athenaeum

Although too many images try too hard to flatter the eye, the fever
or fervor of the paintings in the Athenaeum is catching or fetching.
Elderly subjects gloom from their portraits. The brushstrokes that
flesh them seem richer and surely are thicker than flesh. The back-
grounds recede in browns browner than tropical wood.

I wish I were educated in oils and pastels. I wish watercolor would
wash over me in sobs and sloughs. I wish I understood framing
and being framed. Only someone who has undergone the proper
apprenticeship can enlighten these patriarchs, make them smile.

I turn to the landscapes. Fewer in number and undisciplined in plot.
Small figures conspire. A stream wriggles across a valley. A moun-
tain shrugs with considerable grace. A rider freezes mid-stride, the
horse a hobby horse with tail like a speech balloon. I want to halt
this already static figure and ask how it feels to sport a canvas
backing probably rotten enough to crumble at a touch. I want to
ask the horse how its legs feel, splayed in this unnatural posture.

But I'll leave these questions to art historians. They understand the
upright attitudes of the portraits. They can distinguish one brown
from another. And they probably already know how far that rider
must ride before the painting crumbles into dust.

The Monument

The latest skyscraper offends with its defiant geometry inscribed in brutal planes and striations. The graveyard looks up and pleads. The last tourist drops on all fours and scrabbles in the dirt. He's eating clods, spitting out the grass and swallowing the earth. It doesn't matter who planted this garden of graves, or why the dead lie head to feet, feet to head. Only the glistening skin of the skyscraper can repel the relevant ghosts. Only its acute and unlikely angles can situate the suffering tourist in time and space. But he refuses to look up and enjoy the spectacle of a sneer of glass slicing the pure hard rind of the moon. Such gelatinous events occur almost every night, now that the President has re-elected. Maybe when the criminal charges toughen into bedrock, when the petroglyphs become more legible, everyone will learn to more convincingly blame everyone else. The graveyard sighs a modest but apocalyptic sigh as it ingests the tourist. When he awakens at home in the next century his hands will smell of dead heroes, and his feet will have petrified to agate. Someone will say I told you so; but the skyscraper with its awkward stance will dominate still, its windows oozing spectrums the human eye can't process or even detect.

Ghost to Ghost

The house we've tired of haunting has gone on the market. We'll have to leave, dragging our chains and informing our linen service. The owner is moving to Paris, where her grandchild is a perfect little confection. Being ghosts, we can read the future, and it doesn't look so good. Drugs, unwanted pregnancies, and a sneer that will strip the paint from the walls. But we can't pierce the membrane between life and death to warn our host that she's on a fool's errand. Let's step outside into the sunlight where no one can see us. I love this transparency, don't you? Having doffed our sheets, we're as naked as sandstone, but no one can see us. We can wriggle right up to a courting couple and insinuate ourselves. We can creep into church for the noontime organ concert and slip right through the pipes, smoking into musical shapes only we can appreciate. But let's wander down to the harbor and waft ourselves out to the islands. Don't you enjoy the sea air? Although we lack lungs, it both fills and becomes us, and we become it. A huge cloud of ghost now looms over the harbor, over the city, over the dimpled little islands. No one sees or feels it, no one believes in it. But we too believed in nothing, and look at us now.

The Mustache of Hieronymus Bosch

The light comes off the library façade so heavily it topples the man begging with a cardboard sign. It reads, "Dead Man Strolling Sponsor My Walk." I toss a dollar onto his groans to stifle them. Hieronymus Bosch has become famous again. Everyone's discussing his torrid mustache, his tie-dyed smile. No wonder his paintings hurt so lusciously. One includes this man lying under his cardboard sign. Another includes me as the rump of some huge severed animal. The library, a bastion of culture, roars its approval. Faces beam in its tall windows, the faces of scholars who've spent lifetimes studying the paintings of Hieronymus Bosch. I wonder if they recognize me, or merely approve of the insouciance with which I threw a dollar onto that supine fellow. Shrugging off his flimsy sign, he rises to thank me. God will save, he assures me. The mustache of Hieronymus Bosch twitches with humor. He has already placed us in the paintings of his choice, and no blessing can repaint with enough skill to negate this judgment.

Something After Frank Stanford

Inhaling bus exhaust on Boylston incites something about "white barns of the afternoon," as Frank Stanford put it, a place of excellent overlap. The white barns used to be green. When the deeply Republican proprietor repainted them virgin bride I left New Hampshire weeping.

A dog off leash dares traffic. Everything stops, especially time. I lean into my coffee cup and snort mixed fumes. The dog returns whole and grinning to the curb. I curse its owner with a vision of white barns rumpling like cheap paper. Women in clog heels clomp past. They're eager to reach their offices, where responsible events take responsibility for other events. Everyone benefits.

Meanwhile the "little flowers of the cemetery" bloom without regard for their species, motif, or styles, and creatures cuddle up to other creatures, enjoying the raw light moments before they eat each other. In my cup of coffee, I divine great things, each thing different from every other thing yet subject to undiscovered laws.

Not Drawing Your Portrait

You ask if I'm drawing your portrait. Big filmy eyes, nose strictly Puritan, teeth sharpened by years of bitter speech. Your hair an aerie, your ears trimmed to flatter.

No, I'm not drawing you. I'm sketching the room as if vacant. I like to render the corners oblique, the ceiling and floor acute, the lone window sizzling with sun like fat on a grill.

You're offended that I'm not portraying you in your jaunty summer dress. Little bows on the shoulders. A bodice like the armor plate of an Abrams tank. Your arms too awkwardly attached to render gracefully.

Be glad that dust in the corners and cracks in the walls don't remind me of old acne scars and the wrinkles left by unresolved quarrels. You should appreciate my discretion.

 And no, that squiggle where the walls and ceiling meet doesn't represent your spirit, free of the wreckage at last.

Too Many Screams

Thunder approaches sideways. I've just learned that a friend has starved to death. Although her photographs make her look invincible, her great bulk was deceptive. She shed a hundred pounds in a single withering. Then her organs failed, leaving only a costume of flesh.

Watching the famous historian scribbling in a café I feel how difficult his angle of vision. Although I'm seated behind him, I have a sturdy view of his structure. His seersucker jacket clings like a jilted lover. From the rear, he looks too steep to conquer. His impossible height has stooped over his work but remains frightening. I'm frightened not only by his awkward posture but by the thunder crawling on all fours, dragging hundreds of carcasses.

Maybe my friend swims among those cloudy victims. Maybe her loss of focus defines her more clearly than she's ever before been defined. The historian could research her ascent to the thunder, but he's busy with a study of philanthropy in the late nineteenth century. He has told me how crudely the robber barons exerted their largesse. He described for me the clash of egos that spilled into a thousand rivers and polluted them. How much disease or unease can one era absorb?

Too many screams unravel in the skyways. How can I parse them to identify my friend's? How can an honest historian place them in a context that has no beginning or end?

The Woman in the Flammable Skirt

The woman in the flammable skirt mistakes every gray for ash. Her personal rummage sale precedes her, hundreds of items tagged for instant turnover. Some are organs she coughed up a long time ago, when nuns ruled the earth and converted Jews to salt and pepper shakers. Others are fingernail parings on which famous French poets inscribed the names of the mothers they most hated. Still others are textbooks printed in surf from Cape Hatteras, Cape of Good Hope, Cape Horn, and Cape Cod. This rummage sale often catches fire. So the grays crawl in the roadside ditch and spring into her personal space at predictable but unthinkable intervals. The woman sees herself as a refugee from Oz, Atlantis, or the famous Cream City ghetto. Her body fits so loosely she's afraid it will fall off just to embarrass her before the friction takes hold and her grasp of the earth reifies the husbands she sold to famous universities. Snow drips from a plastic drainpipe. She kneels and drinks and extinguishes her fires from the inside out, and the grays whimper in the ditch, and the flammable snuffs the inflammable in a shower of lit syllables, as if the *Times Book Review* had exploded, leaving no heirs.

The Religious History of America

As you trundle home from church the skyscrapers along the avenue sway in the wind. You think they resemble lilies bobbing on stems, or drunks nodding at the curb, but I think they're unlit torches that when night falls will flare into life and illuminate places you've always wanted to go. Today's sermon eased you into the sleep that eluded you last night. Your bones creaked and the hymnal fell to the floor. The preacher spoke of plenty and multitudes, and wrought iron implements of torture favored by his favorite martyrs. You think love is the spirit that moves the universe but ask any corpse how dark the dark becomes behind the sightless eyes, how far from one star to another.

Your footsteps, slick in sandals that reveal your violet toenails, slap along the sidewalk with a jaunty rhythm fresh from the islands. Which islands? Don't you know? Those tucked somewhere below Antarctica, where flowers shaped like bullhorns regale the spicy breeze. No one lives there because undiscovered; no one dances, sings, or paints hearty watercolors. But the disembodied rhythm has crept around the planet's subtle curves to infect you, and you act out the shyest impulse step by step.

No one except me notices how your shadow of pure alloy drags veils of dust as you progress. Only I care that the daylight moon sickens into the smallest cinder of pure white ash. The preacher warned that the reckoning would come with all four feet planted firmly on the world. You didn't hear because asleep, but when we rose for the final hymn you blinked yourself lively and sang so hard you nearly dislocated your jaw. Now like a boulder rolling lopsided along the avenue you thunder yourself home, every step a triumph.

Trailing far behind, I observe no one observing you and wonder how many fear the Second Coming without realizing that it has come—a slop of drool on the sidewalk, a clapping of sandals, and a smile so absent it drags the unwary eons and eons from their birth.

4.

One Anodized Moment

In the parking garage at dawn
the rows of cars nose the lean
moon setting over the suburbs.
I lie back and listen to ticks
of engines cooling. The air,

although it's already November,
is sultry enough to spoon and eat.
Driving this far this early
has warped me to fit a space
I usually don't occupy.

Later I'll share this space with you
and your frankly remodeled outlook.
We'll stroll in the Public Garden
past the great bronze Washington
and sit beneath your favorite tree.

We'll approach each other like children
and pretend our lives haven't passed
in gales of debt and politics
but have birthed themselves over
and over until perfected.

But for one anodized moment
here in the parking garage
the noon settling in the west
is a hole through which I could pass
to reach the innocence beyond.

Angels Lifting the Skylight

Every silence has eloped.
The trees along the avenue
droop to anoint pedestrians

with fibrous little passions.
Traffic flusters at stoplights,
then proceeds with a sneer.

Looking from your perch above
the city's most tender scenes
you allow your gaze to go naked

in the latest Italian style.
I could name the people passing
five floors below, name them

after characters by Dickens
or Austen or Thomas Hardy.
I could amuse you by comparing

the lions of the public library
with loners who prowl the parks
to meet stray priests or lawyers.

But rain sweeps the view so clean
my chubby little metaphors
would seem as out of place as farm

animals loose in the streets.
What can we do with radio-
active elements in our smiles?

Can we trigger fission or fusion
and harness terrible energies
to improve our private moments?

Down the avenue the steeples
of the cathedral prod the clouds
to awaken sleepy deities.

Umbrellas blossom and bob
along, empowered by curses.
Retreating from the window,

we flop on the unmade bed
and stare at the ceiling in hopes
of angels lifting the skylight

to honor us with a presence,
the only possible presence
we couldn't mistake for ourselves.

Dinner with the Critic

Invited to dine on choice
inorganics, we're conversing
with a movie critic whose work
appears in thick anthologies
no one reads in the bathtub.
She claims that the snake-like form
of outdated celluloid matters,
insinuating into the mind like
a great pale underground worm.
Now digital shucks that effect
and skates across the surface
of perception with a shiver
of eerie but pointless recognition.
We don't quite understand her,
but admire the hinge of her jaw,
which seems better lubricated,
smoother than most. Maybe
closely observing Jack Nicholson
has loosened her bones just enough
to render her slightly more supple
than the average dinner guest.
The first dish is gritty enough
to spread on an icy highway.
The hostess in her sateen gown
beams in the overwrought colors
of Rock Hudson and Doris Day.
The critic nods with conviction.
She reviews three movies a week
and hates them, hates the acting,

the script, and the camera work.
Every week writing her column
she must find three different ways
of expressing the same dry hate.
The server places plates of mush
before us. The critic observes
that something flaccid died for us
and for the crimes of the cinema.
Do we eat this with fork or spoon?
The critic regards us with interest,
catching our conversation frame
by frame with a mental camera
that years ago ran out of film.

In the Goodwill Basement

Junk in the Goodwill basement
gloats with the true pride of kitsch.

Flowered, enameled, molded
to grace the average homestead,

these objects defy description,
but attract with those subliminal

powers only art possesses.
I've never bought such a thing,

but you browse with the ardor
of a scholar of pop culture,

your officious gaze probing
for Elvis Presley or Beatles cast

in ceramic or rubbery vinyl.
I wish I could involve myself

in these shelves of cheap décor,
but plastic penguins and vases

painted with misbegotten roses
fail to hold my eye for more

than a second or two. While
you examine a large serving tray

decorated with mealy faces
supposed to be the Rolling Stones,

I spot a man stealing the Virgin
Mary, stuffing her in a pocket

sewn inside his coat. Intrigued,
I follow him to the stairs where

he pauses to scan the huge room
before ascending and strolling past

the registers where small change rattles
from creaky old leather purses

and ones and fives form angel wings.
He exits, leaving a stink of crime.

With renewed respect for religion
and caution on the steep stairway,

I return to watch you fondle
a teapot so round and ugly

you'll surely either buy it
or regret it for decades to come.

Coast Guard

Every evening I walk a mile
through late-blooming pasture rose
to a site prescribed by law.

All night I scan the Atlantic
for shock waves, screams of pain,
and foreign or threatening slang.

The distance from here to Spain
hangs in the air, a seascape
painted in many shades of gloom.

The government pays me to scour
the picture-plane for subversive
and competing points of view.

No one creeps down the path
after dark. Too cold for lovers
to roll naked on the beach

with all their loose limbs flailing.
Too dark for runaway kids
or hobos prowling for food.

The ocean slops and gobbles
in familiar if alien tongues.
Sometimes in the corner of one

or the other eye it swerves,
tilts, elongates in ways
I can't write up in the notes

I keep in case anyone cares.
Sometimes it slurs like childbirth.
Sometimes it overflows itself

into the lives of those inert
to its constant dredging and filling.
Mostly it casts itself in hues

too subtle for the human eye,
warping my lack of confidence
to conform to faded horizons.

No security threats occur,
although government officials
drown every night in their sleep.

No one blames me, my pay grade
too degrading. Mackerel snap
all night, clams applaud, and starfish

form asterisks to divert me
from the sea-floor's lack of friction,
the silence of pressurized depth.

Public and Private Monuments

Am I allowed to taste the rain?
On Commonwealth, the English elms
heave up last year's birds' nests
and drop twigs on snooping dogs.
My first architectural walk
in years leads past the statue
of Sam Morison, who greets me
with his placid sailor's hello,
enunciated in clear blue tones
that evoke the sea horizon
complete with a distant squall.

As I trundle past, he waves one
heavy bronze arm and gestures
at the Public Garden where squirrels
frisk among tourists for snacks.
Despite the light rain a mob
surrounds the equestrian
George Washington riding
toward the edge of eternity
where his dental work will flourish
in the finest shades of ivory.

Am I allowed to taste the rain
that you planned on keeping
for yourself? I got out early,
drove seventy miles before dawn,
leaving you to tend the garden
by yourself. Mr. Morison

knew I was coming. Tea with him
years ago on Brimmer Street lingers
with a smell of old brown leather.

Traffic snores down Arlington.
I walk to the corner and cross.
Passing through the iron gate
circling Washington's pedestal
and rambling along the duck pond,
I sneak a couple of tastes of rain
and let it nourish and inspire me
with evolutionary notions
of which you would never approve.

Fourth of July in Pandemic

After dark the sputter and pop
of a few distant fireworks
fail to incite the usual
riot of patriotic drunks.
Pandemic has stifled even
the most ardent baring of flesh
and ego, calming decades
of tingling partisan nerves.

You won't have to phone the cops
and demand they stifle the noise,
or grab the garden hose to snuff
fires sparked by roman candles
or skyrockets gone awry.
I won't have to lie awake
pining to resume the flash
and bang of childhood holidays.

Not much celebration left
to celebrate. Fear of infection
breezes through the villages,
smothers the larger cities
where corpses heap in grisly cairns.
Still, we manage to down a pair
of vodkas and tonics and renew
our febrile discussions of art—

whether its agonies still apply
to a world so self-agonized

that it stares through a blinding mist
and sees only a sectarian
muddle of incomplete forms.
Art is supposed to finish those forms
by coloring and molding them
with dimension, weight and texture.

Or so we agree. The fireworks
cough and flare and abruptly desist
as eleven o'clock arrives.
We almost miss the outrage
of celebrations voiding midnight
when the old New England witches
are supposed to take to their brooms
and soar through our troubled dreams.

Black magic no longer avails.
The night skies have surrendered
all their historical gestures.
Even the bats have gone extinct.
No more vodka, so we flop
on the bed and turn on the TV
and bask in flashes of imagery
too pale to penetrate the skin.

Haystack Rock

You think that posing on the beach
places you in time and space,
Haystack Rock bulking behind you,
a landmark almost large enough
to see from the opposite coast.
The wet sand gleams a stainless gleam.
The few other beachgoers bob
in the distance, shy punctuations.
You expect me to count the teeth
in your smile, each a milestone
on the road from this life to that.
You expect the incoming tide
to honor your barefoot tracks
by enhancing them with foam
and bits of wrack for décor.
Your reasoning warps across time
and the ether to embalm me
in the muddle of rain that follows
every step forward or back
in the general rush of elements.
Did Einstein say anything useful
in the climate of your recurrence,
when you bend like time and touch
your toes in the cloudy light
brimming over the Pacific?
Did he claim that mass contracts
when bodies exert their gravities
in mutually comfortable orbits?
I think mass expands when subjected

to your smile, and the first tremor
of the earthquake that someday will trip
a tsunami fatal to this coast
shudders at the base of Haystack Rock
like a word kept under your tongue.

5.

The Last Concert

The stars dress more formally
since we counted the oak leaves
fallen that drab afternoon.

The atomic hues they exude
endorse the infamous nudes
that step from art museums

to dance to certain tunes scraped
on home-made instruments sporting
one string each. We share a love

of such primitive music, the cries
of cats mating and dog-bark
tuning a chorus in G flat.

By the Charles, as conventional
music fumes from the Hatch Shell,
couples explore each other's seams

and find the weak spots where thread
has rotted in the damp climate.
We watch from a safe distance,

remembering that we've counted
enough oak leaves to carpet
the entire river basin. Two

or three little sailboats flicker
in the cold November wind.
Their bow lights guide them back

to the dock to tie up for night.
The last concert of the year
has set the musicians shivering

before an audience upholstered
with boisterous winter coats.
The stars observe with indifference,

but their formal dress expresses
not only the nudes dancing
in Copley Square despite the cold

but also the rehashed Beethoven
churning beside the river.
We watch from a safe distance,

too old to expose ourselves
to the yellow lamplight, too shy
to let the stars understand us.

We can't process each other
the way those young couples do,
but we can parse the starlight

and read in those various hues
a journal someone has kept for us
in our long, unaccounted absence.

Among the Plane Trees

At dawn the owl's final cry
officiates. You feed the cats
with a better grasp of the present
and note the owl perched, preening
after a night of rendered flesh.
In a day or two I'll discover
an owl pellet under the tree.
Secret bones will repose in it
like the bad dreams of a mummy.

The owl clenches against the day,
composing itself as a figure
braced against a background almost
its pattern and color. Likewise
the language we attempt to share
with each other and the world
dissipates against a background
of similar grunts and sighs and groans.

Even in the Luxembourg Gardens
I heard myself dispersed among
a raucous of wanton phonemes,
The gravel shimmered like ore.
Intersecting paths challenged me.
Benches faced chairs facing benches,
but no one sat. They walked, chatted,
ground me under their fluency.

You wonder why I weigh the cry
of an owl as heavily as the curse
of Genesis. Because that spring
afternoon on the Pavilion
my hands were talons and I clawed
myself raw and raving enough
to plant among the plane trees
with my only prey myself
and all my quarrels resolved.

Stirring the Soup

Cream of tomato, celery,
caramelized onion, peppers.
and a dozen other subtleties.

As I stir with a wooden spoon
the soup regards me with pink
and enthusiastic flesh tones.

After a prelude of bubbles and sighs
it thickens into real soup.
Friends arrive and dump their coats

in the bedroom, and with great chatter
line up with mugs and spoons. Behind
the kitchen window, Cambridge

wrings heavy paws in the rain,
preparing to maul whoever dares
attend Harvard's carol service

with its fluted undergrad choir.
Like terraces of mandolins,
hillsides of banjos, meadows

spiked with trumpets and tubas,
the season prefers music to lust.
The soup requires much stirring

because it congeals like a dream
of roiling among striped bedclothes
with an eager and bell-curved partner.

So I add a cup of water to ease
its distinctions and tender its heat.
The pulse of it can't cool, however—

too random and exuberant.
The crowd also congeals, pressing me
against the range. Too many friends,

some chattering in Quebecois,
others swapping post-biblical tales
rife with divine intervention.

The heat of the soup is the heat
of the body. It doesn't deceive.
I stir so hard I ache all over,

but the soup rewards with aromas
thick enough to immunize me
when I drink the dark urban rain.

A Fish-Goddess

Faces prowling Dutch paintings
the day before Thanksgiving
focus on the nearest masterpiece,
accessible with headphones trickling
digital commentary fresh
from the funnybone of intellect.

The smell of the paint faded
long ago, but the ghost of it
teases memory, parsing nations
to reveal the genius and failure
that have privatized all history.
Meanwhile in your big sweater
you look almost as lifelike
as a portrait by Frans Hals.

Hals didn't paint you, but
some other Haarlem artist did.
In a large cityscape with frieze
of gyrating people, a figure
in brown is obviously you.
Your wry approach to the world
skews the figure toward stage right.
The basket of fish you carry
shines like a packet of bullion.

The painter caught you off-guard,
your expression poised between yes
and no, the swing of your hips

a powerful act of logic.
Admit that you posed for this crowd
scene three hundred and fifty
years ago. Don't deny that fumes
from your rotting fish infest
this hallowed and pricey museum.
The crowd surges around Vermeer.
Two little paintings gleaming
with genius the color of old shoes.
I prefer the crowd scene with you
and your fish basket. The sweep
of your lush sweater brightens
the dim-lit galleries, most patrons
unaware that a fish-goddess
stalks about with pure intent.

Red and White Stripes

Framed in the red and white stripes
of your six pillows, your face
goes adrift, warping into places
I can't enter without mourning
the forty years we discarded
like a cargo of empty oil drums.

The city grumbles to itself
with most of its passions muted
by the buzz of construction sites
and the criminal expressions
of cops in fresh new uniforms.
We should visit the museum

with its Dutch masters blazing
and Goya too angry to paint
but painting anyway, on and on
into black and gray infinities.
We should lunch like typical
elderly couples, late blooming

over delicate little sandwiches
and glasses of oily white wine.
In a few minutes the patter
of your bare feet on the hardwood
will present angles of vision
no one since Adam has enjoyed.

The snore of traffic will become
gossip of epic proportions,
and the stoplights will pause
on yellow for hours at a time.
The cops will almost learn to smile,
creasing their aggressive trousers.

Then you'll fade into distance
rendered geological by habits
we hope to acquire. And then
I'll know why the red and white
stripes of your pillows say nothing
of ordinary blood and flesh.

Poor Echo

The angle at which this puddle
reflects the neighboring houses
suggests how dizzily we all stand
in relation to each other.

The sidewalk looks old and tired.
The narrow grass border tries
to instill a vegetable order
on an otherwise urban moment.

The puddle looks glassy enough
to accept a human outlook,
but no one has placed one's self
in that shallow reflective pose.

Do you dare? I don't. My fear
of my own face prevents me
from assuming Narcissus's role.
I prefer to think of the flower,

of the amaryllis family, common
every spring with yellow and white
blossoms flaunting their sex.
While like Narcissus the Hunter

I admire beautiful objects
I know that I'm not one of them,
and shouldn't be looking in pools
or puddles in dirty urban streets.

Not that I'd fall deeply in love
with an imaginary other while
poor Echo fades in the glen,
leaving only her voice behind.

On the contrary, I'd topple
into the puddle and try to efface
myself in an inch of slick.
You may look if you wish. Your face

hasn't inflamed unholy passions,
as Narcissus's self-beauty did,
but it doesn't engender disgust
or comparison to gargoyles.

Still, the puddle is filthy with
the curbside detritus common
to well-worn pavement even
in this slightly prissy neighborhood.

The angle, though. If we looked
from a slightly different stance
maybe the mirrored houses
wouldn't make us dizzy enough

to recall those old mythologies
that no longer explain why
we assume this or that perspective
to improve our view of the world.

Blue People Reading

Rain nails everything into place.
We can't shift the house to look
south, can't roll our glacial boulders
into patterns, can't relocate trees
to flagellate alternative skies.

The vacant shops in the village
adhere to their indelible plots.
Our neighbors walking their dogs
wear ponchos, raincoats, hats
that fit too tightly to remove.

In each house a large blue person
reads a book of fiery pages.
This keeps the whole house warm
so the children can survive until
the sun revives in naked glory.

The threat will congeal everywhere
until torpor overcomes it.
Someday we'll vaccinate ourselves
against the spoked wheels turning
overhead, fatal chandeliers.

Someday the shops will re-open
with displays that will flatter us
as people of taste and goodwill.
The rain takes after the stone
it weathers absolute gray.

When the seams split to reveal
those parts of us too worldly
for the world to acknowledge
we'll be glad we stayed indoors,
downloading our little egos.

Rain simpers and lisps, pretending
to honor the larger creation.
It doesn't fool us. We huddle
over teacups almost small enough
to drown us in moonless tides.

A Postcard from the Ether

The first shy dusting of snow
looks too naked to threaten us
with its pale, indefinite motives.

It can't elide our visions
of banana trees flourishing
many-fingered hands of fruit

in suburbs littered with wrecks
of nineteen-Fifties Chevys and Fords.
It can't erase our dreams of melons

bowling down sky avenues
broader than aircraft carriers.
It can't persuade us that songs

about summer moonlight sating
the hearts of dancing couples
can't snuff the laugh of the dead

still standing where we left them.
The eagle we saw yesterday
cruising over the river,

scanning for fish while fending off
the racket and teasing of crows,
reminded us how negative light

falls in sheaves despite the grace
and curvature of one's narrative.
The snow changes nothing although

it pretends to. It's a postcard
from the ether, illegible scrawl
of blackmail and threat, nothing

worth reporting to the cosmos,
since already diluted by
that obesity's massive humor.

The Aurora in Amherst

For a moment, the canned goods
in aisle four become the teeth
of something chewing at my heart.
You're chatting up our unemployed
baker friend, whose wool cap pulled
low on her forehead covers
scars of her latest lobotomy,
an act of psychic surgery
she performs on herself daily.
I sympathize with such grim
self-negation, but neither of you
have noticed how aggressive
the canned goods appear, how crisp
their labels, how toxic their contents.
Whatever is gnashing my heart
has been busy for many years.
But in this elongated moment
the fractured winter afternoon
oozes salts, acids, fats, additives,
and processed carbohydrates no one
can ingest without consequence.
I'd like to abandon this cart-full
of goods we can't afford and go home
and sulk with the cats and hope
the pain recedes like high tide.
Instead, leaving you engrossed,
I wander to aisle two and examine
labels on hundreds of bottles
of cheap wine from Australia,

Germany, California, France.
The warmth of the vineyards settles
inside me, relaxes the jaws
clenched around my favorite organ.
I return as the conversation
ends in a burst of laughter
 that reminds me of Squire Dickinson
ringing the bells at two AM,
waking Emily and her sister,
so everyone in Amherst can see
the aurora borealis wrapping
the village in green flannel light.

Stay in Your Lane

Crushing green chemical water
with your flagellant stroke, you steer
dead ahead, curb to curb, lap

after lap, inhaling the vapors
you generate with your power.
You've always been a mermaid.

How often have I drowned inside
the whirlpool of your embrace?
Now with age upon us the slick

of an enclosed and heated pool claims
the better part of your energy,
excluding the smallest distraction.

The heavy institutional tile
looks stoic enough to outlast
the Baths of Caracalla. Ropes

strung through Styrofoam floats
throb like heartstrings as you pass
in a thrashing of elegant limbs.

I aspire to distract you within
but not outside your lane, divert
you so slightly no one will notice.

The other swimmers bob like seals.
They don't take the water as fully
as you do, absorbing its light

so your lane darkens behind you
as if the shadow of some creature,
a guardian spirit, followed.

When you climb dripping into air,
the pool looks bereft. Your shadow
erases itself, filling with green

that smells more of sea-bottom
than of bromine. I admire the fact
of you exposed by your swimsuit,

but wonder that someone who holds
such a massive place in the cosmos
still manages to stay in her lane.